God's Design for You:
A Discovery Tool

Pastor's and Layperson's Edition

Published by

Walking With God Ministries International
P.O. Box 7365
Knoxville, TN 37931

Call:
877-814-1860
865-470-8248

Fax:
865-470-8362

Email:
stevewwgm@aol.com

Written and Compiled by:
Steve Harbin

To order additional copies of God's Design for You (Pastor's and Layperson's Edition), or God's Design for You (Church Planter's Assessment Tool) call:
877-814-1860
865-470-8362 (Fax) or email: stevewwgm@aol.com.

ISBN 0-9722876-3-9

Table of Contents

About the Author

 Dr. Steve Harbin is president of Walking With God Ministries International in Knoxville, Tennessee. He is a noted author, conference leader, revivalist, and pastor. Dr. Harbin is committed to the cause of revival and church planting. His heart is to see the church pursuing a love relationship with God. He is a certified human behavior consultant. Steve lives in Knoxville, Tennessee, where he serves as Senior Pastor of Crosspointe Church. He travels extensively leading seminars, conducting crusades, leadership conferences, pastor's conferences, and prayer retreats.

God's Design for You: A Discovery Tool

The Psalmist declares that you were "fearfully and wonderfully" made (Psalms 139:14). Jeremiah declares that before you were born, God knew you. In other words, God has a plan and design just for you. God has designed you supernaturally—you are one of a kind.

Years ago, Rick Warren, Senior Pastor at Saddleback Valley Community Church in California, stated that every Christian has a S.H.A.P.E.[i] God designed you not only for a relationship, but also for ministry and service. The sum total of your life to date is how God has used events and situations in your life to design you for this one moment in time. To understand your S.H.A.P.E., you need to know your:

Spiritual Gifts (How God has equipped you)

Heart (Passion: What you love to do)

Abilities (What can you do-what comes naturally)

Personality (Your unique design)

Experience (What you have done in the past)

Because each person has a unique design, discovering how God created you can be both exciting and enlightening. Knowing how God put you together and designed you is vital to your spiritual victory. The information contained in this book is designed to help you to understand why you do what you do—in other words, what makes you tick.

My good friend, Mels Carbonnel, says, "What makes you ticks is what ticks you off." Every person has a unique personality that is neither good nor bad. It is what you do with your personality that really matters. It is my prayer that this assessment process will result in a fruitful and rewarding ministry, personal growth and development, and an understanding of why you do what you do.

Enjoy the journey!

Steve Harbin

2004

DISCOVERING SPIRITUAL GIFTS

When you became a Christ follower, God equipped you with a spiritual gift or gifts. These gifts allow you to serve in your unique ministry—a ministry and place of service designed with you in mind. You are special to God, and He wants you to know what your ministry is. It is important for you to understand that gifts are designed for a season. God continually prepares you for the ministry that He has for you at every point in time along your life's journey.

Perhaps you have been a Christ follower for a long time. What God designed for you as a new believer may have been quite different from what He is designing for you today. Just as God gives you unique gifts for specific tasks, He also gives direction for ministry based on your personal growth and development. So as God gives direction for ministry, He also changes and modifies your gifts to meet the challenges awaiting you.

Therefore, it is important for you to profile your spiritual gifts regularly[ii] to gain a clear understanding of how God is leading and equipping you. Spiritual gifts are only one part of the puzzle that reveals your ministry and mission in life. You are a multi-dimensional individual. You also need to look at your passion, personality profile, abilities, and experiences.

For added reading and information, Scripture references are provided. The Apostle Paul addresses the presence of spiritual gifts in three main sections of Scripture: Romans 12, I Corinthians 12, and Ephesians 4. Peter also verifies their existence in I Peter 4:10. Through these sections of Scripture, we learn that all Christians have been given at least one spiritual gift. The purpose of spiritual gifts is two-fold: (1) to unify Christians in their faith and (2) to produce growth within the church, both numerical and spiritual. These gifts are to be used out of love for one another, and in service to one another. We do not choose which gifts we will receive. God bestows them on us through the work of the Holy Spirit.

Not all of the gifts identified in Scripture are used in this inventory. The spectacular gifts (speaking in tongues, interpretation of tongues, and miracles) and some of the non-spectacular gifts (martyrdom, celibacy) have not been included. Although these gifts exist, they are not commonly used in the mainstream of church life. Since God's desire in giving spiritual gifts is to unify His church and produce growth through service, only the service-related gifts are included.

Gifts Definitions and References:

NOTES

Record any thoughts or impressions about your spiritual gifts and you read through the material. Then do your Spiritual gifts profile

1. Apostle/Entrepreneur: Unlike the Apostles of the New Testament, who actually saw Jesus, today's Apostle has a clear vision to start new ministries. These individuals make great entrepreneurs and are strong leaders. They reach out where others may never dare. They demonstrate overwhelming abilities in getting others to follow their leadership. They also have a contagious enthusiasm that crosses all cultural, geographic, and economic boundaries. Relevant Scriptures: Ephesians 4:7-11, 1 Corinthians 9:1-2, 1 Corinthians 12:28-29, Galatians 2:8-10.

2. Administration: This gift enables a believer to formulate, direct, and carry out the plans needed to fulfill a purpose. These individuals focus on team participation, see the big picture, and strive to keep everyone on track. They like to evaluate what needs to be done, design systems to get the job done, and then assign responsibilities to others. Relevant Scriptures: I Corinthians 12:28, Acts 14:23.

3. Discernment: This gift motivates a believer to seek God's will and purpose and apply that understanding to individual and congregational situations.

These persons have the ability to see through confusion and point out possible solutions. They are good listeners but tend to be too critical and too serious. They feel strongly about obeying truth and living by the Scriptures. Relevant Scriptures: John 16:6-15, Romans 9:1, I Corinthians 2:9-16; 12:7, 10, 14.

4.   Evangelism: This gift moves believers to reach nonbelievers and win them to faith in Christ. They want every message they hear to have evangelistic overtones. Missions and outreach are important to them. Relevant Scriptures: Matthew 28:16-20, Ephesians 4:11-16, Acts 2:36-40; 8:26-40, Luke 19:1-10.

5.   Encouragement/Exhortation: This gift moves the believer to reach out with Christian love to others facing personal and spiritual conflict. They bless others with a strong sense of concern. Often trying to encourage others, they are sought out as counselors. They are encouraging, friendly, understanding, and practical. Relevant Scriptures: John 14:1, Romans 12:6,8, Acts 11:23, II Timothy 1:16-18, III John 5-8.

6.   Faith: This gift gives a believer the spiritual eyes to see the Holy Spirit at work and the ability to trust the Spirit's leading, even when the destination is not clear. They trust God in the most adverse circumstances. They believe strongly in the presence and power of God. Relevant Scriptures: Genesis 12:1-4a, Matthew 8:5-16, Mark 5:25-34, I Thessalonians 1:8-10, Hebrews 11:1.

7.   Giving: This gift enables believers to recognize God's blessings and to respond to those blessings by generously and sacrificially giving their resources (time, talent, and treasure). Relevant Scriptures: II Corinthians 9:6-15, Luke 21:1-4, Romans 12:6-8, Acts 4:32-35.

8.   Hospitality: This gift enables a believer to joyfully welcome guests and those in need of food and lodging. They love to provide refreshments or to prepare meals for individuals or groups. They seldom are irritated over last-minute requests to have others in their home or to host a group. They tirelessly serve to make people comfortable. Relevant Scriptures: Romans 12:13, Romans 16:23a, Luke 10:38 and 14: 12-14, 1 Peter 4:9-10, Acts 16:13-15.

9.   Intercession: This gift is found in those who have a passion for prayer. They are compelled to intercede for others, especially for those in distress. They faithfully petition God for specific needs. They recognize that spiritual battles are won in the prayer closet. They are the spiritual glue of every church. Relevant Scriptures: Romans 8:26-27, John 17:9-26, 1 Timothy 2:1-2, Colossians 1:9-12; 4:12.

10.   Knowledge: This gift allows a believer to receive supernatural revelations of certain truths, gaining specific information that could only be known from God. This is not an amplification of human knowledge, nor a gift of knowing a lot of things. It is an insight from God. Relevant Scriptures: 1 Corinthians 12:7-8; 8:1-2.

11. Leadership: This gift is evident in those who demonstrate an ability to influence others. It gives a believer the confidence to step forward, give direction and provide motivation to fulfill a dream or complete a task. Believers with this gift are often results-oriented and driven, but are also great motivators. Relevant Scriptures: Romans 12:8, John 13:13-17, 21:15-17, II Timothy 4:1-5, Hebrews 13:17.

12. Mercy: This gift motivates a believer to feel deeply for those in physical, spiritual, or emotional need and then act to meet that need. Relevant Scriptures: Luke 7:12-15, Luke 10:30-37, Matthew 25:34-36.

13. Pastor/Shepherd: This gift gives a believer the confidence, capability and compassion to provide spiritual leadership and direction for individuals or groups. They see their service as one of maturing others. They have strong feelings about spiritual health in the Body of Christ. Relevant Scriptures: 1 Timothy 3:1-13; 4:12-16, 2 Timothy 4:1-2, Ephesians 4:11, 1 Peter 5:2-4.

14. Service/Ministry (Helps): This gift enables a believer to work gladly behind the scenes in order to fulfill God's work. Those gifted in this area are motivated by a strong sense of need, and they feel that "someone has to do it." Relevant Scriptures: Luke 23:50-54, Romans 16:1-16, Philippians 2:19-23, 1 Corinthians 12:28, Acts 6:1-3, Romans 6:1-2.

15. Teaching: This gift enables a believer to communicate a personal understanding of the Bible and faith in such a way that it is clearly understood by others. Interested in

research, believers with this gift like to dig into background information and enjoy presenting what they discover. They love to study. Relevant Scriptures: I Corinthians 12:28, Matthew 5:1-12, Acts 18:24-48.

16. Wisdom: This gift allows the believer to sort through opinions, facts and thoughts to determine the solution that would be best for an individual or community of believers. Relevant Scriptures: I Corinthians 2:6-13, James 3:13-18, II Chronicles 1:7-11.

17. Prophecy: Prophets today are not the same as prophets of old. The Old Testament prophet spoke the literal Word of God. Today, people with this gift seek the truth through prayer and God's Word with a similar seriousness and straightforward attitude. There are no gray areas for those with the gift of prophesy. They share the truth no matter what anyone thinks. When under the control of the Holy Spirit, today's prophets often find themselves pointing the way, declaring specific truth, or standing up for something significant. Relevant Scriptures: Romans 12:6-8, 1 Corinthians 12:7-10, 28-30; 14:1-5; 30-33, 37-40, Ephesians 4:11.

INSTRUCTIONS: SELF-ASSESSMENT INVENTORY

This questionnaire will help you identify your God-given gifts. While there are many spiritual gifts, this evaluation covers the gifts used in daily life to do the work of Christian ministry. Every Christian has a dominant gift, and many possess more than one. Through this analysis, you will find out which areas are not as strong and which areas are dominant. Then, you can begin to concentrate on developing your dominant gift further as you exercise it in daily life and in your local church ministry.

For each of the questions that follow, circle the number that corresponds with the response that most closely matches how you see yourself. Responses are:

> 1 = Rarely True
> 2 = Infrequently True
> 3 = Occasionally True
> 4 = Frequently True
> 5 = Consistently True

Creative exercise: To get a clearer picture of your spiritual gifts, ask a person who is close to you to score the inventory with you. Their perception of your strengths may be useful in clarifying your gifts. After you respond to each question, turn to the scoring grid to analyze your results.

SPIRITUAL GIFTS PROFILE

1. I like to build projects, businesses, or ministries from scratch   1   2   3   4   (5)

2. When presented a goal, I immediately think of steps needed to achieve results.   1   2   3   (4)   5

3. Sometimes I am asked if a direction under discussion is in agreement with God's will and purpose.   (1)   2   3   4   5

4. I like to share my testimony with unsaved people   1   2   3   4   (5)

5. I am moved by those who are wavering in faith because of conflict or sorrow.   1   2   3   (4)   5

6. I can see great things happening in my congregation and am not derailed by the pessimism of others.   1   2   3   4   (5)

7. I am blessed by God each day and gladly respond to these blessings by giving liberally of my time and money.   1   2   3   4   (5)

8. I enjoy welcoming guests and helping them to feel at ease.   1   2   3   4   (5)

9. I know that God hears and responds to my daily prayers.   1   2   3   4   (5)

10. My study of scripture gives me unique knowledge   1   2   3   4   (5)

11. I am a take-charge person. When others follow my direction, the goal or task will be completed.   1   2   3   4   (5)

12. When I see a person in need, I am moved to assist them.   1   2   3   (4)   5

13. People have come to me for spiritual help and it has developed into a long-term relationship.   1   2   3   4   (5)

14. I become irritated when people sin   (1)   2   3   4   5

15. I tend to do much more than I am told to do   1   2   3   4   (5)

16. I want to express my faith by helping others to discover the truths contained in the Bible.   1   2   3   4   (5)

17. When direction is needed at work or in the congregation, I am generally asked for my opinion.   1   2   3   4   (5)

18. I am willing to move elsewhere in order to start something new.   (1)   2   3   4   5

19. I tend to motivate others to get involved.   1   2   3   4   (5)

20. I read between the lines when people are talking.   1   2   3   4   (5)

21. I can share the gospel with a total stranger.   1   2   3   4   (5)

22. I am often compelled to share advice.   1   2   3   4   (5)

23. I enjoy being around people who pray a lot.   1   2   3   4   (5)

24. I manage my time and money so that I am able to give much of it to the work of the church or other organizations.   1   2   3   4   (5)

25. I am often asked to open my home for small group gatherings or social occasions.   1   2   (3)   4   5

26. I often become so absorbed in my prayer life that the door bell or phone can ring and I will not hear it.   (1)   2   3   4   5

27. I feel compelled to learn as much as I can about the Bible and faith.   1   2   3   4   (5)

28. When I am in a group, others will often look to me for direction.   1   2   3   4   (5)

29. I feel an urgency to provide housing for the homeless, food for the starving, comfort for those in distress.   1   2   3   4   (5)

30. I have responsibility for providing spiritual guidance to an individual believer or group of believers.   1   2   3   4   (5)

31. I discern evil before others do.   1   2   3   4   (5)

32. When I turn out the lights, take tables down, work in the kitchen or put chairs away, I feel that I have served the Lord.   1   2   3   4   (5)

33. My great joy is to communicate Biblical truth in such a way that it becomes real and clearly understood by others.   1   2   3   4   (5)

34. When a challenge is presented, I am usually able to identify an appropriate solution.   1   2   3   4   (5)

35. I adapt well to other cultures   1   2   3   4   (5)

36. I can accomplish numerous tasks in a day.   1   2   3   4   (5)

37. I am able to detect things that are not spiritual.   1   2   3   4   (5)

38. I love to hear evangelistic type messages   1   2   3   4   (5)

39. I really enjoy counseling others   1   2   3   4   (5)

40. My trust in the Spirit's presence is a source of strength for others when we encounter times of personal crisis.   1   2   3   4   (5)

41. When I receive money unexpectedly, one of my first thoughts is to share this gift through the church.   1   2   3   4   (5)

42. I enjoy meeting new people and becoming acquainted with them.   1   2   3   4   (5)

43. Believers have asked me to pray for healing in their lives, and I have experienced God's healing power.   1   2   3   4   (5)

44. Not one day would be complete without Bible study and reflection on its meaning.   1   2   3   4   (5)

45. People have said that they like to work with me because the task will be successfully completed.   1   2   3   4   (5)

46. People are surprised by how comfortable I am with those who are suffering in mind, body or spirit.   1   2   3   4   (5)

47. I am motivated to provide spiritual leadership to those who are on a faith journey.　　　　1　2　3　4　(5)

48. I do research to share truth rather than to gain personal information and knowledge　　　　1　2　(3)　4　5

49. People come to me for help in applying Christian faith and values to personal situations.　　　　1　2　3　4　(5)

50. Students have told me that I can take the most difficult idea or concept and make it understandable.　　　　1　2　3　4　(5)

51. People say I demonstrate an unusual amount of wisdom.　　　　1　2　3　4　(5)

52. My heart's desire is to start new churches or ministries　　　　(1)　2　3　4　5

53. I enjoy organizing thoughts, ideas, hopes and dreams into a specific plan of action.　　　　1　2　(3)　4　5

54. My faith requires me to seek out God's will and purpose in all of life's circumstance.　　　　1　2　3　4　(5)

55. I enjoy being with non-believers and encouraging them to grow in faith and commitment.　　　　1　2　(3)　4　5

56. When I know someone is facing a crisis, I feel compelled to provide support and care.　　　　1　2　3　(4)　5

57. I tend to judge people by their faith.　　　　(1)　2　3　4　5

58. Being a poor steward of finances is sinful.　　　　(1)　2　3　4　5

59. I like to invite people in need to stay in my home.　　　　(1)　2　3　4　5

60. I believe prayer is the greatest power given to believers.　　　　1　2　3　4　(5)

61. My study of the Bible has helped to others in their faith journey.　　　　1　2　3　4　(5)

62. I know where I am headed and I am driven to bring others with me.　　　　1　2　3　4　(5)

63. Solving problems is my main concern. (1) 2 3 4 5

64. I seem to look for spiritual lessons in
    everything I encounter. 1 2 3 4 (5)

65. I proclaim truth as it comes from God. 1 2 3 4 (5)

66. I like working behind the scenes to ensure
    that projects are successful. 1 2 (3) 4 5

67. I search to new insights on life as I study
    God's Word. 1 2 3 4 (5)

68. I see easily the difference between truth and
    error. 1 2 3 4 (5)

69. I get excited about new mission world
    around the world. 1 2 3 4 (5)

70. Some of my best work is done under
    pressure 1 2 3 4 (5)

71. I can tell when people are insincere 1 2 (3) 4 5

72. I am able to convey the Gospel message to
    non-believers in ways that they are able to
    understand easily. 1 2 3 4 (5)

73. Those who are struggling with life questions
    have come to me for guidance and help. 1 2 3 4 (5)

74. I know God answers prayer. 1 2 3 4 (5)

75. I am concerned about the financial needs of
    others (1) 2 3 4 5

76. A neat/clean home is not as important as
    being available to others. 1 2 (3) 4 5

77. People say I am a "Prayer Warrior." 1 2 (3) 4 5

78. I like to learn things that most people do not
    know. 1 2 (3) 4 5

79. It bothers me when people sit around and
    do nothing. 1 2 3 4 (5)

80. I can't say no to legitimate needs. 1 2 3 (4) 5

81. I love leading groups toward spiritual
    maturity 1 2 3 4 (5)

82. I can be stubborn and difficult to convince. 1 2 (3) 4 5

83. I would rather do a job myself, rather than delegate it to others. (1) 2 3 4 5

84. I have a tendency to prepare too much material for my group. (1) 2 3 4 5

85. I tend to make wise choices and decisions. 1 2 3 4 (5)

SCORING GRID: After completing your Spiritual Gifts Profile, place your response (1-5) in the appropriate numbered box below. Total up each category to see your areas of giftedness. This inventory is designed to begin the journey toward discovering your spiritual gifts. Keep in mind that it is not a scientific instrument. Over time, your perceptions will be validated by others and confirmed through prayer and service. Identify your spiritual gift cluster, then list the gifts in the space provided.

						Total
Apostle/Entrepreneur	5 — 1	1 — 18	5 — 35	1 — 52	5 — 69	17
Administration	4 — 2	5 — 19	5 — 36	3 — 53	5 — 70	22
Discernment	1 — 3	5 — 20	5 — 37	5 — 54	3 — 71	19
Evangelism	5 — 4	5 — 21	5 — 38	3 — 55	5 — 72	23
Encouragement/Exhortation	4 — 5	5 — 22	5 — 39	4 — 56	5 — 73	23
Faith	5 — 6	5 — 23	5 — 40	1 — 57	5 — 74	21
Giving	5 — 7	5 — 24	5 — 41	1 — 58	1 — 75	17
Hospitality	5 — 8	3 — 25	5 — 42	1 — 59	3 — 76	17
Intercession	5 — 9	1 — 26	5 — 43	5 — 60	3 — 77	19
Knowledge	6 — 10	5 — 27	5 — 44	5 — 61	3 — 78	23
Leadership	5 — 11	5 — 28	5 — 45	5 — 62	5 — 79	25
Mercy	4 — 12	5 — 29	5 — 46	1 — 63	4 — 80	19
Pastor/Shepherd	5 — 13	5 — 30	5 — 47	5 — 64	5 — 81	25
Prophet	1 — 14	5 — 31	3 — 48	5 — 65	3 — 82	17
Service/Ministry	5 — 15	5 — 32	5 — 49	3 — 66	1 — 83	19
Teaching	5 — 16	5 — 33	5 — 50	5 — 67	1 — 84	21
Wisdom	5 — 17	5 — 34	5 — 51	5 — 68	5 — 85	25

With which gifts have you been blessed? Discovering the answer to that question requires the following:

- Prayer: Seek the Holy Spirit's guidance while evaluating your gifts.
- Study: Become familiar with the Scripture references, gifts definitions, and how each gift functions within the Body of Christ. This will provide you with a solid foundation from which to evaluate your gifts further.
- Self-examination: Explore your feelings about each of the spiritual gifts in your cluster. Examples of how each gift may be used in the church are provided below. As you read these examples, ask yourself how you feel about the types of ministry activity identified for the gifts in your cluster. You should expect to feel fulfilled as you use your gifts.
- Tracking Your Results: As you use your spiritual gifts, pay close attention to the results produced through your response to God's call. You can expect to experience positive results from using your gifts.
- Listening for Affirmation: As you use your spiritual gifts, listen for affirmation from other Christians. They will recognize and confirm your spiritual gifts through genuine expressions of approval and thankfulness for a job well done!

Reading Your Graph

To determine which gifts are most like you, circle the top three or four boxes with the highest scores. Take notice of the gifts that are most intense. The higher your score is on the profile, the more closely that gift describes you. Also notice your next highest and lowest plotting points to learn more about your overall gift tendencies.

BEHAVIOR DISCERNMENT INVENTORY

Each of us has strengths and weaknesses that make us effective in some situations and not so effective in others. There is a special blend in knowing ourselves and knowing our Lord that helps us get along with others. We often study about knowing Christ. However, we study very little about knowing ourselves. Yet, healthy, positive relationships please God and bring us closer to Him and to each other.

The ability to predict how we react in certain situations is of enormous value as we attempt to work with, serve, influence, and communicate with others. This is true whether we are working in the secular or church world.

Past behavior is the best predictor of future behavior. And behavior is influenced by a number of complex factors such as personality, emotional state, physical health, skill development, personal experiences, values, and motivational needs.

Once you discover yourself, you can anticipate behavior in certain situations and can serve and relate to others better. This Behavioral DISCernment Inventory can help you understand how and why you and others behave in one way or another.

Through this process, you will gain insight into what makes you tick as a person. You will also learn how to apply these concepts to improve relationships with the unique people in your groups (at home, work, or church). This inventory will enable you to discover and define how you view yourself and how you want others to see you.

This inventory is not an exam or a test. There are no "right" or "wrong" answers. This tool helps you to discover and analyze your own behavioral style, seek work in an environment that is conductive to your success, and adapt your behavior to particular situations to create more productive relationships with others.

Completing the Behavioral DISCernment Inventory

Read Carefully: In the inventory on the next page, read across the columns from left to right. In descending order, rank the selections in each of the 25 categories that best describe your behavior at work or in school. Use a "4" for the statement that is <u>most</u> like you, a "3" for the statement that is <u>often</u> like you, a "2" for the statement that is <u>occasionally</u> like you, and a "1" for the statement that is <u>least</u> like you. Write a number in the column under the # sign. You must use the numbers 4, 3, 2, and 1 only once in each row of answers.

SAMPLE							
My personality is mostly…							
Forceful	3	Expressive	2	Restrained	4	Compliant	1

My personality is mostly…							
	#		#		#		#
Forceful	1	Expressive	3	Restrained	2	Compliant	4
Strong Minded	4	Emotional	1	Satisfied	3	Careful	2
Direct	1	influential	4	Accepting	3	Correct	2
domineering	1	attractive	2	willing	4	Precise	3
Determined	4	Stimulating	1	Even-Tempered	3	Meticulous	2
Demanding	2	Captivating	4	Patient	3	Timid	1
Self-Reliant	1	Companionable	4	Kind	2	Conscientious	3
Persistent	2	Playful	1	Self-Controlled	3	Agreeable	4
High Spirited	4	Talkative	1	Good-Natured	2	Conservative	3
Impatient	1	Convincing	4	Contented	3	Resigned	2
Aggressive	1	Good-Mixer	4	Gentle	2	Respectful	3
Takes Risks	1	Poised	3	Accommodating	4	Conventional	2
Argumentative	1	Confident	4	Relaxed	2	Cooperative	3
Restless	1	Inspiring	4	Considerate	2	Well Disciplined	3
Courageous	3	Optimistic	4	Sympathetic	1	Diplomatic	2
Positive	3	Charming	4	Lenient	2	Exacting	1
Adventurous	2	Enthusiastic	4	Loyal	3	Controlled	1
Will Power	3	Entertaining	4	Good Listener	1	Humble	2
Competitive	4	Fun-Loving	1	Obedient	3	Tactful	2
Vigorous	2	Persuasive	4	Neighborly	3	Cautious	1
Outspoken	3	Eloquent	4	Reserved	1	Strict	2
Decisive	2	Animated	4	Obliging	1	Accurate	3
Assertive	3	Sociable	4	Steady	2	Orderly	1
Bold	3	Outgoing	4	Moderate	1	Perfectionist	2
Bottom Line	2	Responsive	3	Helpful	4	Consistent	1
W=	53	X=	83	Y=	60	Z=	55

Add all the numbers in each of the columns (W,X,Y, and Z). The total of all four columns should equal 250.

Scoring Your Profile

Instructions:

1. Check the accuracy of the # totals for each of the W, X, Y, Z columns. All four columns, when totaled together should equal 250.
2. Now plot the number from each column onto the graph below.
3. Draw lines to connect your D, I, S, and C points, moving from the D to the I to the S, and then to the C.
4. Circle the highest point on your graph. This is your core style.

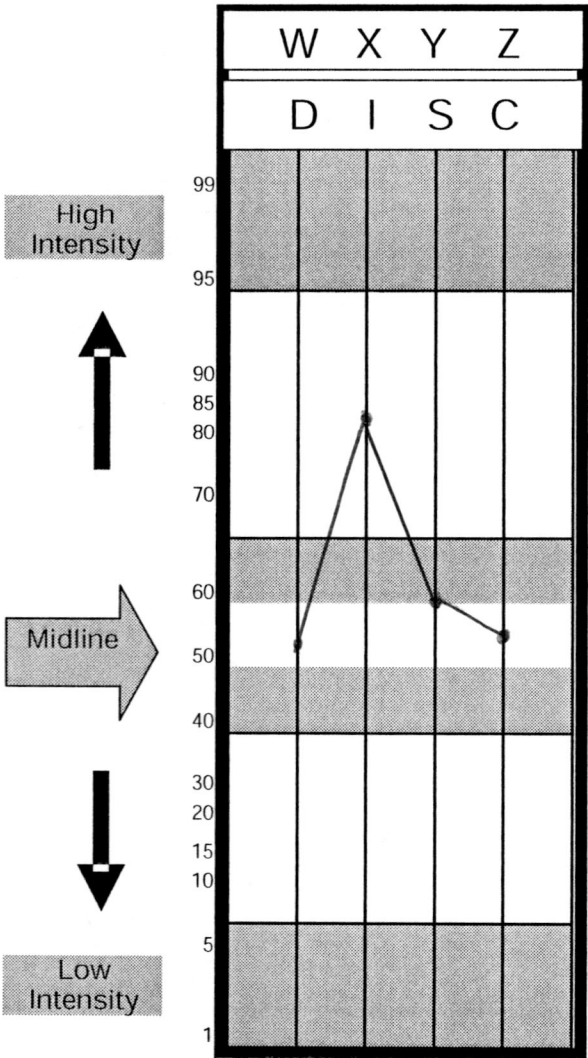

Your Profile Graph

Your Profile Graph

Your DISC profile is a wonderful description of your personality style. You can see the intensity of each of the four personality styles. Each point above the midline identifies your behavioral strengths.

The behavior of most of the population is a combination of two or more styles above the midline. This is called your behavioral blend. If you have only one point above the midline, you have a pure behavioral style. Take a look at your highest point and where it falls in relation to the other three points on your profile graph. All of your points above the midline contribute to your behavioral blend.

Write your behavioral blend: I/S

Which letter corresponds to the highest point on your graph? I

Which letter corresponds to the highest

Dr. William Marston devised the theory of human behavior in 1928 as a result of extensive research. During this research, he identified four major behavioral patterns that are present in all people, but to different degrees.

Over the years, others have built on his four-dimensional theory of personality, making it one of the most popular systems for teaching people about behavior styles. This profile system is based on the following factors:

- Dominant:

    The drive is to be in control, to achieve results. The basic intent is to overcome.

- Inspirational:

    The drive is to express, to influence, and to be heard. The basic intent is to persuade.

- Steady:

    The drive is to be stable and consistent. The basic intent is to support.

- Compliant:

    The drive is to be right, sure, and safe. The basic intent is to avoid trouble.

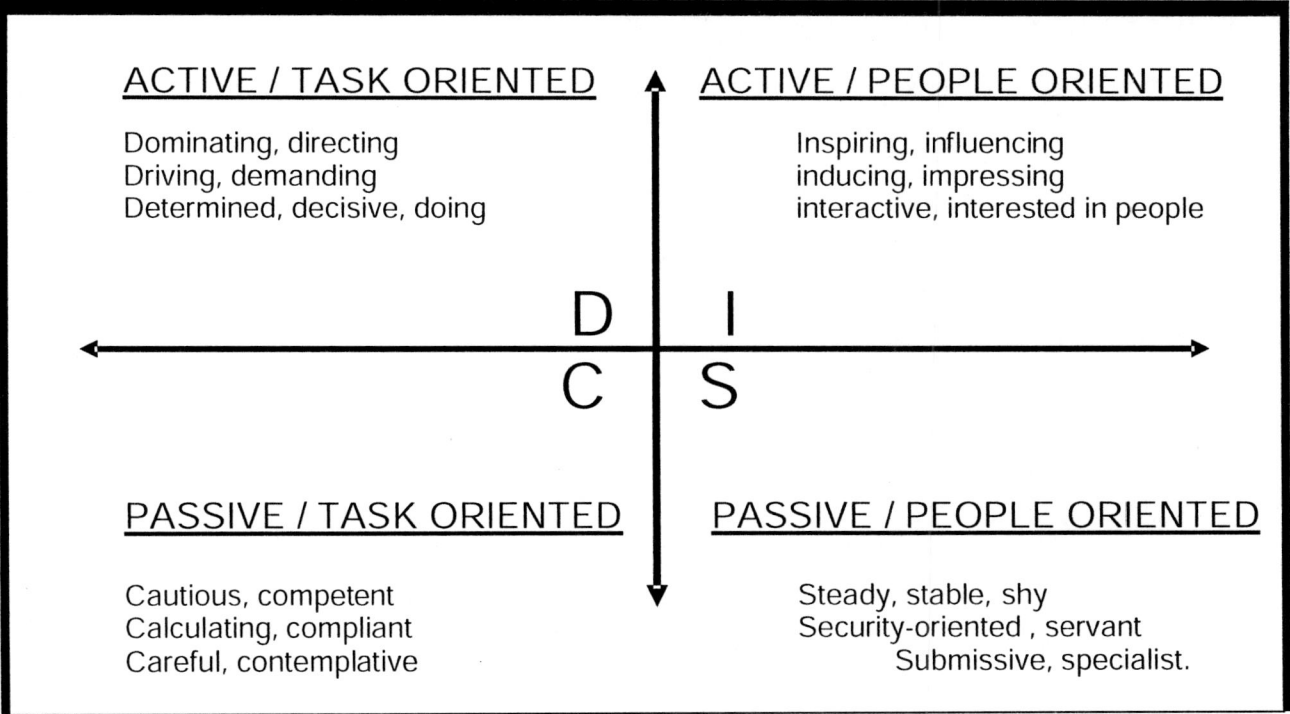

WHAT DISC MEASURES

Dominant (Choleric)

Other Terms: Direct, Demanding, Decisive

Emphasis: Controlling the environment by overcoming opposition to achieve desired goals.

"D" type personalities are self-starters who get going when things get tough. The higher the "D" value, the more active and intense an individual will be in trying to overcome problems and obstacles. The lower the "D" value, the greater the tendency to gather data prior to making a decision.

"D" personalities thrive on competition, tough assignments, heavy workloads, pressure, and opportunities for individual accomplishment. If you have a "D" personality, you are discontent with the status quo. You are a real individualist and very self-sufficient. You demand a great deal from yourself and others.

Needs to Learn: You need people. Relaxation is not a crime. Some controls are needed. Self-control is most important. Learn to finish well.

Biblical Examples: Paul and Sarah

Inspiration (Sanguine)

Other Terms: Expressive, Inspiring, Influencing, Persuader

Emphasis: Creating the environment by motivating and aligning others to accomplish results.

"I" type personalities thrive on social contact, one-on-one situations, and freedom from control and details. They are friendly, outgoing persuasive, and confident.

If you have an "I" personality, your basic interest is in people. You are poised and meet strangers well. People seem to respond to you naturally and you usually have a wide range of acquaintances. Your innate optimism and people skills help you get along with most people.

Needs to Learn: Time must be managed. Deadlines are important. Too much optimism can be dangerous. Being responsible is more important than being liked.

Biblical Examples: Peter and Ruth

Steady (Phlegmatic)

Other Terms: Amicable, Submissive, Stable, Security-oriented, Supporter

Emphasis: Maintain the environment to carry out specific tasks.

"S" type personalities thrive in a relaxed, friendly atmosphere without much pressure. They seek an environment that offers security, limited territory, predicable routine, and credit for work completed.

"S" personalities are amiable, easy-going, warm-hearted, loving, and neighborly. If you have an "S" personality, you are even-tempered, low-key, and generally content with the status quo. You are prone to leniency with yourself and others. The higher the "S" value is, the more you prefer to start and complete one project at a time. The higher the "S" value is, the more resistant to change you become. The lower the "S" value is, the faster the pace and the greater your desire is for change.

Needs to Learn: Change provides opportunity. Discipline is valuable for life. Risk taking is sometimes necessary.

Biblical Examples: Moses and Hannah

Compliant (Melancholy)

Other Terms: Conscientious, Competent, Analytical, Cautious

Emphasis: Structuring the environment to produce products and services that meet high standards.

"C" type personalities thrive on order, pre-determined methods, tradition, and conflict-free atmospheres. They like ample opportunities for careful planning without sudden changes.

"C" personalities are precise and attentive to detail. If you have a "C" personality, you prefer to adapt to situations to avoid conflict and antagonism. You try to do whatever others want you to do. Naturally cautious, you prefer to wait and see which way the wind is blowing. Once your mind is made up, you are very firm in adhering to procedures.

Needs to Learn: Total support is not always possible. Thorough explanation is not everything. Deadlines must be met. The more optimistic you are, the greater your chance is for success.

Biblical Examples: Thomas and Esther

POSSIBLE STRENGTHS
DISC PROFILE

		D	I	S	C	
D/I Perceptive	99	Driving	Captivating	Self Controlled	Perfection	I/D Diplomatic
D/S Gets Results	95	Revolutionary	Inspiring	Accommodating	Precise	I/S Personable
	90					
D/C Decisive	85	Innovative	Persuasive	Tolerant	Thorough	I/C Confident
	80					
	70	Confident	Participator	Good Listener	Methodical	
	60	Upbeat	Optimistic	Dependable	Adaptable	
MIDLINE	50	Midline	Midline	Midline	Midline	
	40	Conservative	Outgoing	Alert	Firm	
	30	Unassuming	Accurate	Flexible	Single-minded	
	20					
C/D Supportive	15	Willing	Reflective	Active	Unconventional	S/D Controlled
	10					
C/I Disciplined		Down-to-earth	Reasonable	Energetic	Self-determining	S/I Concentrates
	5	Non-Demanding	Diagnostic	Intense	Free Spirited	
C/S Conscientious						S/C Determined
	1	Submissive	Questioning	Dynamic	Fearless	

This graph plots the possible strengths that are characteristic of each of the four personality behavioral traits. As you plot your behavioral blend, notice the relationship patterns that develop between each of the plotting points. Anything above the midline is a strong behavioral pattern and plays a role in your personal behavioral patterns. This helps you to determine "why" you do "what" you do. Remember, what makes you tick is probably what ticks you off.

POSSIBLE LIMITATIONS
DISC PROFILE

		D	I	S	C	
D/I Too Blunt	99	Argumentative	Self-Promoting	Apathetic	Overly Dependant	I/D Too Agreeable
D/S Never Satisfied	95	Autocratic	Superficial	Unresponsive	Evasive	I/S Verbally Pushy
	90					
D/C Domineering	85	Antagonistic	Overly Optimistic	Too Lenient	Worrisome	I/C Too Optimistic
	80					
	70	Hard	Overly Confident	Overprotective	Defensive	
	60	Hurried	Poor Listener	Non-Demonstrative	Too Compliant	
Midline	50	Midline	Midline	Midline	Midline	
	40	Hesitant	Reserved	Restless	Opinionated	
	30	Withdrawn	Blunt	Impatient	Stubborn	
	20					
C/D Worrisome	15	Over-Cautious	Suspicious	Assertive	Immovable	S/D Too Patient
	10					
C/I Poor Delegator		Unassuming	Distant	Tense	Rebellious	S/I Overly Possessive
	5	Fearful	Negative	Impetuous	Defiant	
C/S May Over manage						S/C Rigid
	1	Intimated	Introvert	Restless	Radical	

This graph plots the possible weaknesses that are characteristic of each of the four personality behavioral traits. As you plot your behavioral blend, notice the relationship patterns that develop between each of the plotting points. Anything above the midline is a strong behavioral pattern and plays a role in your personal behavioral patterns. This helps you to determine "why" you do "what" you do. Remember, what makes you tick is probably what ticks you off.

BEHAVIORAL STYLE OVERVIEW

Likes an active environment where they can have authority

The High "D"

1. High achiever

2. Impatient

3. Direct

4. Desires change

5. Does many things at once

6. Must be confronted

7. Iron-willed

8. Self-regulating

9. Overriding

10. Decisive

Greatest Concern or Worry: Being taken advantage of

"The Leader"	
What Others Appreciate	**What Others Dislike**
General Relationships:	
Strong willed	Unsympathetic
Productive	Insensitive and inconsiderate
Decisive	Sarcastic
Practical	Unforgiving
Visionary	Domineering
Optimistic	Argumentative
Born leader	Opinionated
Strong need for change	Proud
Must correct wrongs	Impatient
Not easily discouraged	Has difficulty relaxing
Independent	Not complimentary of others
Self-sufficient	Unemotional
Won't give up when losing	
In Small Group Relationships	
Exerts sound leadership	Tends to dominate others
Establishes goals of others	Too busy for family and friends
Motivates others to action	Holds others to high standards
Knows the right answer	Tends to use people
Organizes others	Doesn't need other's approval
Has little need for friends	Hard to say "I'm sorry"
Will work for group activity	Feels always right
Excels in emergencies	Possessive
Ministry and Work	
Goal oriented	Low tolerance for error
Sees the complete picture	Expects others to manage details
Organizes well	Bored by emotional stories
Seeks practical solutions	Rash decision maker
Moves quickly to action	Rude or tactless
Delegates work	Manipulative and demanding
Insists on productivity	Ends justify the means
Stimulates activity	Workaholic
Thrives on opposition	Demanding of others

The High "I"

Likes an active environment where they can be accepted

1. Expressive

2. People-oriented

3. Chaotic

4. Hopeful

5. Encouraging

6. Influencing

7. Enthusiastic

8. Persuade

9. Demonstrative

10. People person

Greatest Concern or Worry: Loss of social approval

"The Conversationalist"

What Others Appreciate	What Others Dislike
General Relationships:	
General Relationships:	Undisciplined
Outgoing and charismatic	Restless
	Disorganized
Warm and friendly	Unproductive
Talkative	Naïve
Compassionate, demonstrative	Self-centered
General and sincere	Exaggerates
Good sense of humor	Dwells on trivia
Enthusiastic and expressive	Egotistical and obnoxious
Good on stage	Controlled by circumstances
Wide-eyed and innocent	Weak-willed
Lives in the present	Forgetful
In Small Group Relationships	
Is liked	Unreliable
Turns disaster into humor	Seems phony to others
Is the life of the party	Selective listener
Relates well	Center stage
Thrives on accomplishments	Dominates conversation
Admired	Answers for others
Apologizes quickly	Inconsistent
Spontaneous	Makes excuses
Ministry and Work	
Volunteers	Would rather talk than work
Thinks up new activities	Forgets obligations
Looks great on the surface	Doesn't follow through
Creative and colorful	Confidence fades fast
Has energy and enthusiasm	Undisciplined
Performer	Priorities out of order
Does things in a flashy way	Decides by feelings
Inspires others	Easily distracted
Charming	Wastes time talking

The High "S"

Likes an active environment where they can be appreciated

1. Trustworthy

2. Team-player

3. Person of substance

4. Family-oriented

5. High level of trust

6. Possessive

7. Resists change

8. Adapts slowly

9. Capable

10. Steady

Greatest Concern or Worry:
Loss of security

"The Family"	
What Others Appreciate	**What Others Dislike**
General Relationships:	
Likeable and diplomatic	Unmotivated
Efficient and organized	Spectator
Dependable	Selfish
Conservative	Stingy
Reluctant leader	Self-protective
Loyal	Indecisive
Patient and well balanced	Unenthusiastic
Quite, but witty	Avoids responsibility
Keeps emotions hidden	Fearful
Practical	Too compromising
In Small Group Relationships	
Makes a good friend	Unchangeable
Is not in a hurry	Doesn't organize well
Can take good with bad	Takes life too easy
Doesn't get upset easily	Dampens enthusiasm
Good listener	Stays uninvolved
Dry sense of humor	Indifferent to plants
Has several close friends	Judges others
Compassionate	Sarcastic and teasing
Ministry and Work	
Competent and steady	Not goal-oriented
Peaceful and agreeable	Lacks self-motivation
Has administrative ability	Hard to get moving
Mediates problems	Resets being pushed
Avoids conflicts	Discourages others
Good under pressure	Observer
Finds the easy way	Lethargic

The High "C"

Likes an active environment where they can have control

1. Receptive

2. Precise

3. Questions

4. Diagnostic

5. Controlled

6. Submissive

7. Detail person

8. Capable

9. Capable

10. Obsessive

"The Thinker"	
What Others Appreciate	**What Others Dislike**
General Relationships:	
Analytical and idealistic	Moody and negative
Contentious thinker	Critical
Loyal	Rigid and legalistic
Sensitive	Self-centered and touchy
Self-sacrificing	Revengeful
Self-disciplined	Persecution prone
Serious	Unsociable
Eccentric	Theoretical and impractical
Talented and creative	Has false humility
Artistic or musically gifted	Has selective hearing
	Introspective and low self esteem
Philosophical or poetic	Tends to be a hypochondriac
Appreciative of beauty	
In Small Group Relationships	
Sets high standards	Unrealistic goals
Wants everything done right	Too meticulous
Picks up ate everyone else	Becomes a martyr and sulks
Sacrifices for others	Lives through others
Encourages scholarship	Socially insecure
Makes friends cautiously	Critical and unforgiving
content to stay in background	Holds back affection
Avoids receiving attention	Hard to forget hurts
Ministry and Work	
Schedule-oriented	Not people-oriented
	Depressed over imperfections
Perfectionist	
High standards	Chooses difficult work
Detail oriented	Compulsive planner
Economical	Prefers analysis to work
Sees the problem	Self depreciating
Finds creative solutions	Hard to please
Wants to finish a project	Sets unrealistic Standards
Likes charts, graphs, figures	Deep need for approval

Greatest Concern or Worry:
Criticism, change in situation or circumstances

UNDERSTANDING AND INTEGRATING YOUR BEHAVIOR BLEND

DISC describes the four basic personality types of behavior. Most people have personalities that are a combination of these four types of temperaments. Please note: no one type of personality is better than another. There are no bad personalities verses good personalities. Simply put, most people have a blend of these style dimensions in varying degrees of intensity.

Integrating your behavioral blend will give you a better understanding of your unique personality by describing your natural strength, emotions, goals, methods of influence, value to work, church, or small group, and even fears. Understanding your spiritual gifts, strengths, limitations, and ministry contributions (along with your personality temperament) can help you understand your place in the Body of Christ.

Only you can decide if a pattern fits your concept of yourself. However, if you have accurately portrayed yourself in the DISC profile, you will be able to say, "Hey, this sounds like me!"

Instructions:

1. Using the graph of your DISC profile, look at your plotting points above the midline. Determine your primary characteristic (highest plotting point) and your secondary characteristic (2nd highest plotting point). If a third plotting point is above the midline, make note of that also.

2. Once you have determined your highest plotting points, go to the DISC category describing your highest plotting point.

3. Find the column referencing your behavioral blend. Note the pattern name of your behavioral blend. You will find an explanation of pattern names on the pages that follow.

Dominant: Choleric, the person in Charge

<u>Pure D: Visionary Doer</u>... Exhibits a powerful, individualistic approach, especially towards new challenges and opportunities. Frequently demonstrates high ego strength. Desires excitement and sometimes jumps into new adventures before thinking them through. Makes demands on people and situations in order to accomplish a goal. Likes to win at any cost.	<u>D/I: Determined Influencer</u>... Bottom-line, high-powered individual with a unique ability to take a creative idea and make it serve practical purposes. Likeable person who is motivated by completing tasks and building relationships. Excited by activity, energy, variety, and change. This is an active personality style.
<u>D/S: Driving Achiever</u>... Objective and analytical in style. Can be fiercely independent and competitive. Derives motivation from internal rather than external forces. A driving desire to achieve overrides consideration of others, causing this person to appear distant and non-caring. Focuses more on achieving a goal rather than on the people who help achieve the goal..	<u>D/C: Confronting Challenger</u>... Determined students and defiant critics who want to be in charge, while collecting information to complete tasks. Drivers who drive others and themselves, they can be dominating and caustic. Their greatest fear is that they will not be influential or that they will fail. A challenger who will speak the truth in any situation.
<u>D/I/C: Inspirational Controller</u>. Demanding, pressing, and competent. Tends to be less people-oriented but more focused on the task at hand. Wants things done correctly, completely, and in a timely manner. Works to resolve problems, combing accuracy with quick thinking. Under pressure, tends to express feelings without allowing others to share opinions	<u>D/I/S: Visionary Director</u>... Has vision and people skills and exhibits an ability to move people and tasks in a forward direction. Is energetic and sociable. In a stressful situation, acts with determination and perseveres to the end. Is impressing, demanding, and stabilizing at the same time.

Inspiration: Sanguine, the conversationalist

<u>Pure I: Influential Communicator...</u> Are impressive individuals who are extremely active and excitable. Friendships and approval are important to them. They can become careless and disorganized. Their communication skills are above average. In a difficult situation, this person is likely to express every feeling they possess or withdraw to an emotionally safe place. Inspiring and flattering, they use their enthusiasm to generate a friendly team-oriented environment.	<u>I/D: Inspirational Persuaders</u>... Are super salespersons. Exhibit outgoing personalities with a high interest in people. Have the ability to gain respect and admiration from varied types of individuals. Thrive when given assignments requiring mobility and challenge. Want people around them to communicate efficiently and effectively. Appear to be overconfident, aggressive, or pushy.

I/C: Competent Assessors... Are inspirational yet cautious. Are observant of details as well as the unique value of people. Complete tasks with enthusiasm and optimism. Encourage others. Are excellent judges of character, and easily trust those who meet personal standards. Can be persuasive and too concerned about winning. Are often impatient and critical.	**I/D/C: Inspirational Leaders**... Demonstrate a high task orientation. Enjoy being around others. Are friendly and involve others in projects and tasks, but also want things done right. Influence others using strong people skills and an ability to reason and be logical. Are not bystanders, but are constantly involved. Desire the excitement that comes from new adventures and meeting new people.
I/C/S (I/S/C): Cautious Influencers... Exhibit high-energy, excellent communication skills, and sensitivity. Are direct, friendly, and enthusiastic. Prefer to be informal, but are talkative. Desire to be team members and like to know exact expectations before starting new projects. Are dominant leaders if the parameters of authority are clearly defined. They influence people with their knowledge of facts. Have unique abilities to analyze people and situations.	**I/D/S: Motivational Reformers**... Are sociable and friendly. Like to drive situations and be leaders. Are caring and accepting of others. Concentrate on the tasks at hand until they are completed. Keep their personal limitations in check by asking for help when necessary. Function well at the level of team leader and/or team player. Use directness to solve conflicts. Are sensitive to others and attempt to create environments favorable to everyone.

Steady: Phlegmatic, the family

Pure S: Persistent Technicians... Are seen as modest, sociable, dependable, and determined. Are not easily swayed once their mind has been made up on any matter. They set their own pace and stick with it. Are steady and consistent, preferring to deal with one thing at a time. Secure, non-threatening surroundings are important to them. They make the best friends because they are so forgiving. Are motivated by sincere opportunities to help others.	**S/D: Investigative Achievers**... Are determined, logical, tenacious, and rigidly independent. Amiable but usually aloof, decisive and quite deliberate; they are reflective but not hesitant to voice opinions. Like to follow leads, chase clues, dig for facts, and uncover hidden meanings. They analyze problems and evaluate circumstances objectively. Dominate with patience. Though fiercely independent, they enjoy working as part of a team. They are results-oriented without a sense of urgency. To them, effective performance is more the result of long, hard work than from flashes of insight or inspiration. performance is more the result of long, hard work rather than flashes of insight or inspiration.

S/I: Steady Advisors… Are sensitive and inspirational. Others see them as easy-going, friendly, relaxed and independent. Are nice people who pose no threat and are impossible not to like. People approach them with their problems and they are willing to listen. People are naturally drawn to them because of their warmth, sympathy, empathy, and understanding. Their self-confidence, poise, mildness, persistence, and devotion to people make them likeable. Motivated by opportunities to share and shine, they induce others to follow. They would be more influential, however, if they were more aggressive.	S/C: Steady Peacemakers… Appear to others as quiet, amiable, predictable, self-controlled, practical and down-to-earth. Seek the familiar and maintain relationships with a few relatively close friends. Are cool-headed, reflective, and considerate, and "wear well" with others. Steady and contemplative, they like to search for and discover the facts. Are systematic and sensitive to the needs of others, but can be critical and caustic.
S/D/C: Contemplative Strategists… Are seen as positive, cool, steady, and systematic. Are direct and straightforward. They like to tell it like it is. Are intellectually curious and challenged by difficult problems requiring brainpower and logical analysis. Are reserved and reflective, devoted to standards, procedures, precedent, and traditional methods. They avoid unnecessary risks. Are conventional, diplomatic, and worrisome. Are rarely satisfied in their search for the best answer. Are often seen as perfectionists.	S/C/I: Advocates…Like to do things right, impress others and stabilize situations. Are not aggressive or pushy. Enjoy large and small crowds. Are good with people and prefer quality. Are sensitive to criticism; therefore, they are sensitive to what others think about them and their work. Can do things well, but are poor at quick decision-making. Are stimulated by sincere, enthusiastic approval and logical explanations. (See also S/I/C and C/I/S: Competent Mediators.)

Compliant: Melancholy, the thinker

Pure C: Logical Thinkers… Their predominant drive is careful, calculating, compliant, and correct behavior. When frustrated, they can overdo it or become the exact opposite. They need answers and opportunities to reach their potential. Tend not to care about the feelings of others. Can be critical of themselves and others. They like projects that stimulate their thinking. Make decisions slowly based on facts and logic. They ask the "how and "why" questions.	C/D: Competent Designers… Are able to initiate change and improvements because of their administrative skills. Sometimes feel they are the only ones who can do a job correctly. Have a tendency to get bogged down and not allow others to help. Under pressure, they come across to others as aggressive or stubborn. It is important for them to be sensitive to the needs of others around them in order to insure a positive environment. They value accuracy and precision. High standards are maintained in all aspects of their work life.

C/D/S: Competent Contemplators... Are cautious, stable and determined. Are more task-oriented, but care about people on an individual basis. Are detail-oriented and have high standards for themselves and others. They don't like to speak in front of crowds. Prefer to get the job done right through small groups. Tend to be more serious. Others often misunderstand them as being insensitive because they are selective and analytical in their relationships. Natural achievers, they need to be friendlier and less critical.	C/I: Competent Assessors... Are inspirational yet cautious. Are observant of details as well as the unique value of people. Complete tasks with enthusiasm and optimism. Encourage others. Are excellent judges of character, and easily trust those who meet personal standards. Can be persuasive and too concerned about winning. Are often impatient and critical. (See also I/C: Competent Assessors.)
C/I/S: Competent Mediators... Like to do things right, impress others and stabilize situations. Are not aggressive or pushy. Enjoy large and small crowds. Are good with people and prefer quality. Are sensitive to criticism; therefore, are sensitive to what others think about them and their work. Can do things well, but are poor at quick decision-making. Are stimulated by sincere, enthusiastic approval and logical explanations.	C/S: Precision Specialists... Have a precise, detailed, and stable nature. Are systematic thinkers who tend to follow procedures in their personal and professional lives. Are highly tactful and diplomatic in nature. They painstakingly require accuracy in work and maintain high standards. They like people, but prefer having only a few close friends. "Exactness" describes them, and criticism is equated with failure. They are consistent, cautious and seldom take risks.

Special Level Patterns

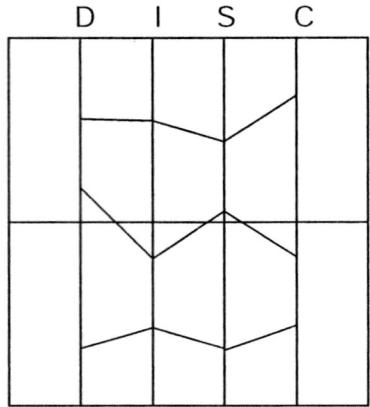

Straight Level Pattern along the mid-line: This behavioral blend occurs when all four plotting points are extremely close together, centered on the mid-line of the profile grid. This may indicate that this individual is a people-pleaser and wants everyone to be happy. It may also indicate they have difficulty answering the profile questions because they do not know how they should answer them. Not knowing how to answer the questions may leave them frustrated.

Straight Level Pattern above the mid-line: Two possible indicators are present when the level pattern is here. First, it may indicate the person is extremely adaptable to all types of situations, much like Chameleons. Second, this may indicated a strong desire to overachieve.

Straight Level Pattern below the mid-line: This may simply occur because the individual is not sure how to respond to challenges. They are likely to compromise, concede, and comply with accepted and expected practice.

YOU AND OTHERS: THE BEHAVIORAL BLEND AND BUILDING TEAM

It has been said, "No man is an island." Though it is a well-known statement, it has practical and long-term ramifications in building relationships. As an entrepreneur, you will be building extensive relationships with people from all walks of life, with all types of behavioral blends. To maximize the results of your launch in Kingdom work, develop a relational recipe for success.

ABILITIES ASSESSMENT TOOL
Your Natural Makeup, Abilities, and Experience

Abilities are the natural talents that are part of who you are. Some people have a natural ability with words. Others have natural athletic abilities. Some are naturally good with numbers, while others are good with people. This Abilities Assessment Tool is designed to help you discover your abilities and your best place of ministry in Kingdom work.

1. Describe a time you successfully started a project, ministry, or business.

2. Write about an obstacle someone placed in the path to your dream.

3. Describe ways you have motivated a person or persons to commit to a goal.

4. Tell about someone with whom you developed a relationship who is lost or unchurched.

5. How does your spouse feel about your call to ministry service?

6. Describe your devotional life or quiet time.

7. What recent training events have you attended?

8. Describe what you delegate to others.

9. Describe a specific prayer request God answered.

10. List every ministry, job, work, and skill you have employed in your lifetime. Use the back of this sheet, if necessary.

11. On a separate sheet of paper write out your salvation experience and call to ministry and/or church planting.

YOUR PASSION PROFILE
What Drives You?

1. What has been the most successful accomplishment in your life?

2. What activity or ministry generates your greatest emotional response?

3. What has been your greatest disappointment or fear (in life or ministry)?

4. For what are you willing to take the highest risks?

5. If you could do anything for God, what would you do?

6. About what issues or causes do you feel most strongly?

7. Describe your emotional feelings when thinking about starting a major new project.

8. Describe someone in the community you have personally helped to meet a need in their life. How did you meet that need?

9. Describe a situation when your ministry expectations were high, but the outcome was unexpectedly disappointing. Describe your response to that disappointment.

GETTING TO KNOW YOUR TEAM

Team Profile Graph

	D	I	S	C
99				
95				
90				
85				
80				
70				
60				
50				
40				
30				
20				
15				
10				
5				
1				

Compare up to five behavioral blends of your team members. To observe the possible differences in the profiles, use different color ink pens or markers.

Once you have transposed everyone's graphs, begin to notice the differences. Always remember, differences are not bad. They simply illustrate the dynamics at work within the team.

OBSERVING THE TEAM BUILDING GRAPH

Observations:

1. Number of high "D" personalities above the midline: _____
    Indicates active, determined, task-oriented behavior.

2. Number of High "I" personalities above the midline: _____
    Indicates more active, inspiring, task-oriented behavior

3. Number of High "S" personalities above the midline: _____
    Indicates passive, stable, people-oriented behavior

4. Number of High "C" personalities above the midline: _____
    Indicates passive, cautious, people-oriented behavior

5. Who are the High "D" personalities?

6. Who are the High "I" personalities?

7. Who are the High "S" personalities?

8. Who are the High "C" personalities?

9. Is the team more Active or Passive? _____

10. Is the team more Task- or People-oriented? _____

11. What is the personality profile of this team? _____

12. What are the strengths of this team?

13. What are the weaknesses of this team?

14. As you look at your team, what are your greatest concerns or fears?

Endnotes:

[i] Rick Warren, The Purpose Driven Church, page 370, Zondervan Publishing, 1995

[ii] The Spiritual Gifts Profile and Behavior DISCernment Inventory were specifically designed for this book. However, there are several of leading organizations that offer a variety of spiritual gifts inventories and DISC profiles. The author recommends the following organizations: Uniquely You, Blue Ridge, GA; Team Resources, Atlanta, GA; The Institute for Motivational Living, New Castle, PA.

Printed in the United States
41249LVS00003B/573-774